Poppet, My Poppet

poems by

Ann Chinnis

Finishing Line Press
Georgetown, Kentucky

Poppet, My Poppet

ACKNOWLEDGMENTS

The author wishes to thank the editors of the following journals or anthologies
in which these poems first appeared:

"My Mother's Land O Lakes Sweet Cream Butter Recipe Tin" and "Ode on
Disappointment", *Nostos: Poetry, Fiction, and Art*
"Doxology to My Mother's Manners", *OpenDoor*
"Dreaming in Reverse", *Drunk Monkeys*
"The Contextualist", *Speckled Trout Review*
"The Chinoiserie Wallpaper", *Sky Island Journal*
"The Ozarks", *Landscapes & Cityscapes*

Deep gratitude and appreciation to the Writers Studio, which has been a
place of community, support and learning. Special thanks to my teacher Lisa
Bellamy and to my classmates in New York City Advanced Poetry who were
life-lines during the pandemic and whose feedback was precious as I birthed
most of these poems. Special thanks to my current teacher Phillip Schultz
and my fellow writers in Master Class who challenge and inspire me with the
power and beauty of their writing. And to my poetry pen pal, Val Jonas, thank
you for your friendship and writing wisdom.

Publisher: Leah Huete de Maines
Editor: Christen Kincaid
Cover Art: Carrie Stump, Carrie Michelle Photography,
    Carriemichellephoto.com
Author Photo: Carrie Stump, Carrie Michelle Photography,
    Carriemichellephoto.com
Cover Design: Elizabeth Maines McCleavy

Order online: www.finishinglinepress.com
        also available on amazon.com

Author inquiries and mail orders:
Finishing Line Press
PO Box 1626
Georgetown, Kentucky 40324
USA

Contents

My Mother's Land O' Lakes Sweet Cream Butter Recipe Tin

rests on sacred ground where orange Formica nestles
gold Hot Point range: recipes typed on white file cards
from soup to nuts. It begins with *Pam's Episcopal Punch: In a large*
punch bowl, combine one quart orange ice with 1 bottle vodka and
2 quarts chilled ginger ale. Add a block of ice when the first guest
arrives. Serves 15-20. Typically, 10. Mad chemist,
my mother fumigates her punchbowl with Wright's Silver Polish until
the kitchen reeks of diesel. She punishes the ladle
with grey flannel until every print is lifted, extracts
a just-washed punch glass from my soapy hand, spins it
in the sun, prisms crystal into color: her laugh a champagne flute
clinking *(but never the rim, so thin and prone to break).*
See how water spots cast rainbows? She washes them
again. You always know where you stand. As each churchly
guest arrives, she exchanges overcoat for punch glass. Would that
every daughter be her aide de camp; catch her wink
as she flings you their wrap; your bed a coat rack, a bivouac; your
room, a proving ground, me—her private, privvie to her sortie's
aim to right some hallowed wrong.

Land O' Lakes certified sweet cream butter, Minneapolis, Minnesota, scores
93 butter points; you can read that on the tin. My mother has no
truck with butter that is not FINE, SWEET, and CLEAR. Should butter or
daughter fail to please, there is the crush of sterling butter press,
the welt of her *silence, scorn, so disappointed, pointless, how you throw*
yourself away. You always know where she stands. Next is the
Spa Vichyssoise Soup: Serve very cold, with a hit man's sangfroid,
scope trained on target. Her frustration mounts
with *Williamsburg Cheese Straws. I have never had much success with cutting*
into strips. Use a whiskey jigger to press into biscuits and place a pecan
in the middle. What daughter hasn't bucked her mother's blade to face
the jigger in her middle?

My mother is Marquis de Lafayette: Yorktown laid to siege
with *Tropical Hot Fruit Compote for 100: 16 cups each of apricots, peaches*
and pineapple chunks, 32 cups of Bing Cherries, 16 oranges, 16 lemons
and 8 cups of brown sugar (light). And a scrape of nutmeg. Do not
scant the sugar. I am her Rochambeau, pommeling Cornwallis
with peach pits. From the first parallel, she unveils
her howitzer, *the Shrimp Thermidor: 40 lbs. of cooked shrimp, mushrooms,*
flour, milk, butter, salt, cheese, and sherry. Or white wine,

if preferred. You could bask in 40 shelled lbs. of her fierce approval. *You*
    have left not a shred of vein on those shrimp; Eat one,
go ahead! Sterno stews under the chafing dish; my mother and I, warming,
    chafing. She always knows where she stands. *They will remember*
the Thermidor when the vote is called.

Mamie Eisenhower's Million Dollar Fudge
    is her guests' white flag of surrender, marshmallow cream
creeping from warm cocoa center, meandering around obstacles
    of pan. *Take a lesson, my stubborn dear.* So why
am I still her sentry, her standard bearer, long after her sword has
    been buried beside her? Because in her Land O' Lakes
Sweet Cream Butter recipe tin is my alpha and omega. How I have
    felt her lips on my cheek, watched her limp up another podium,
    rage while others prayed. I have rocked with her under a peach sunset,
    when she could no longer speak. With a straight edge, in fountain pen,
    my mother ruled the last card for me in her Land O' Lakes Sweet Cream
    Butter recipe tin. It is otherwise blank, not penned
as an invitation—more drawn like a gauntlet.

Doxology to My Mother's Manners

My Mother's manners are an apology for her Ozark roots; thank you notes
nibbed on monogrammed cards, swift and gift specific, serious

as a Vanderbilt gilding her audience, but home-spun too, penning barefoot
as she yarns you about her one room school, windows rattling from the train

to St Louie, the kids waving like crazy to a hazy face, counting boxcars.
Her manners are a ruse. She never says stupid unless delivered as

a catechism; *Stupid is as stupid does*, each time you back into
the same mailbox. My mother's manners are as steadfast as her

Aqua-Net hair, more resolute than her starched sheets. Even when
you're grown, move from home, she will lay your coat on her bed

with the guests', after sherry send you off with the rest saying,
Don't be a stranger. They are a lasso of truth; how she hands you

punch in a crystal cup, lulls you into spilling your guts. *What do
you think of your father's new wife?* My Mother's manners are

a bribe; a German Chocolate cake baked from scratch, coconut
and fingertip grated into icing, delivered in my Pinto to Lenten

Luncheons when she campaigned for Senior Warden. Her manners
are a Trojan horse sporting a periwinkle beret down K Street to Vestry

meetings, me in red Keds, us scheming to upend the church's creeds
on ordaining women priests. They are a sucker punch in black leather

gloves from October through March, not one day later, pinching my
arm when I half-kneel in church. Before she takes the dais she puts

herself down *Good-Old-Wishy-Washy-Mom* and you think she's eating
from the palm of everyone's hand. She's a battering ram, clears

her throat, raps her gavel: *the Distinguished Deputy from Delaware
is Out of Order. Please sit down.* Her manners are trotlines set for the vote

with silver butter press on the left, salt cellar, right: her bait, pounds of shrimp
Thermador (lemon removes the stench on your hands) swallowed hook, line

and dogma by her guests. My mother's manners are a psalm, a call to action.
I end her battle hymn in benediction. The last train from St. Louie echoes
up the tracks. A distant whistle. Three-short. One-long.   Unanswered calls.

Dreaming in Reverse

Faster. Fast. The face's fractured fragments
realign. Her jaw snaps back in place, locks
itself home, safe between its bony condyles.

The woman on the floor at the foot of the stairs
rises in the air. Her vision clears; the stars retreat
like Perseids at moonrise. Her blood unpuddles

from the baseboard at the linen closet's door.
The woman's teeth dive from the folded sheets
on the bottom shelf, surprised by their speed, skid

under the crooked space where the door fails
to meet the floor, and with a hard bounce, vault
into their sockets. The woman's split lip seals

like a tire plugged by a roadside Samaritan. The linen
closet door opens, pushes the woman's head away,
propels her body up the stairs. This is where we thought

she was rearranging furniture in the night. Her
limbs helicopter her up the stairs where the little girl
waits. Halfway up the stairs, the woman's peach

nightgown settles, no longer bunched like a needy
child around her neck. At the landing, the woman
stands. In the dark, she jerks her floating foot from

the air and plants it. Barefoot, she walks backwards
to the little girl's bed room. The girl's nightmare
is mist in the chimney. She sleeps, no longer thirsty.

Her "Mommy could you get me some water" echoes,
a quantum thought in the event continuum of the girl's
life, that blackhole from which nothing remembered

will escape. This is where I stop dreaming in reverse:
the mother crawling into bed with the daughter,
the quilt pulling itself up from the foot of the bed, each square
holding them there, arresting their orbits like glue.

My Mother's Mink Coat

I didn't know that the day Roe v. Wade was
overturned by the Supreme Court, defeated,
I would clean out my closet, and my dead mother
would be standing there sifting through my

windbreakers, looking for her mink coat—walnut
with obsidian strips from shawl collar to calf hem. She
leans her face into the pelts, inhales her Femme
by Madame Rochas Perfume. She is perching

a periwinkle beret on her Aqua Netted hair. She licks
her thumb to rub a smudge off her patent leather
handbag. How many German chocolate cakes
did she bake from scratch for church Lenten Luncheons?

How many podiums did she climb to convince
the Episcopal church to ordain women? So many
chalices, their rims smeared by lips forbidden
to bless them—their lipstick and Listerine,

their Beechnut and sausage. After each communion
she headed to the Parish Hall to slice her German
Chocolate cake, dip punch and speak softly about things
she loved—full moons, her children, religions that treasured

everyone. When the punch glasses were spotless
and the Parish Hall floor had been swept, my mother
drove home, hung her mink coat in the louvred
closet, took her lined pad to the attic, penned

another sermon on justice, booked another
hotel room near a parish where she could deliver
a German chocolate cake and her speech.
Twenty years later, when the Sports Medicine attending

stonewalled me for a job ,"Don't bother applying
here—women physicians are a distraction to our
highly trained athletes", my mother shared this
story. On the day my grandmother drove my nearsighted

mother from their Ozark home to college in Virginia, my
mother sat on her glasses, broke the nosepiece, arriving
East, bashful and blind. She and my Granny walked arm
in arm to the dorm; my mother sat down on her bed, did

the only thing she could with no glasses—she began
reading, established herself as smart and impenetrable,
an instant sorority commodity. When my Granny brought
her a new pair of eye glasses a week later, my mother
smiled, kissed her, and kept on reading.

My Mother's Apotheosis

Tonight, I am looking at my Girl Scout sash,
16 badges sewn on in trios—except the last,
Cooking, hidden on the tip that sits
on your hip—where you rest your hand
when you are ripe for a fight, if a boy

mentions that badge. I was most proud
of my Nation's Capital Patch, even though we lived
in Virginia. My joy each year—our trip to the Capitol—
my God, its white dome looming as the school bus
crept down Constitution Avenue, idled at those

front steps—365 from the basement to dome, one
for each day of freedom—back then the entrance
wasn't fenced off with wire, no National Guard.
We filed off the bus, climbed the marble stairs
and Troop 1848 traipsed around the rotunda—me

dizzy from looking up 140 feet at the Apotheosis
of George Washington ascending to heaven, holding
hands with Victory and Fame, thirteen maidens cleaning
his feet—the original states—pedicurists. I thought
something smelled fishy when I saw Washington greeting

War, Science, Marine, Commerce, Mechanics and Agriculture
in heaven—they looked like Boy Scout badges—nothing like
CrossStiching, HomeMaking, BikeRiding, CookieSelling,
LetterWriting, StoryTelling, FindingFourLeafClovering.
I came home, told my mother I wanted to be a Boy Scout not

a nail tech, and why couldn't I carry the cross in church
like my brother, be a page in the US House of Representatives,
go to an all-male college up north, dress like a hippy, be
an Obstetrician like my uncle? My mother invited me
to sit in the high-backed chair facing her desk, said it
was custom—not gospel, that women couldn't be priests
in the Episcopal Church, not that my mother wanted
to be a priest—she pulled for the underdog—said there
are two kinds of campaigns, one to get yourself
elected, the other to conquer your oppressor—said

that is why she bakes German chocolate cakes
from scratch for Lenten luncheons—gets her
in the door through the kitchen—and once you are
elected as president of the Church Women—you set
your sights higher, fight a 30-year war, maybe

more, before you die a female priest places
the host in your hand. I closed my eyes, saw My
Mother's Apotheosis, her holding a German Chocolate
cake on a platter, surrounded by
Victory, Cunning, Justice, Equity, even Revenge.

My mother asked me what war I cared enough to wage.
I said the Girl Scouts weren't worth the ammo. I loved
an underdog too—asked her if I could enlist as
a Youth for Nixon, would she drive me
to the Willard Hotel to stuff envelopes, answer

phones, look out the 9th floor window onto
Pennsylvania avenue at the White House and practice
my inauguration address?

Ode on Disappointment

White rocking chairs faced hunched pinions in rocked gully,
potted Saguaro cactus wobbled on cobalt tiled table—
we had wanted desert. The Red Rock before us,
like a blow torch the welder ignited: sunset.

We turned to each other, toasted our trip,
you in black Ferragamo shoes, a two-piece navy knit suit,
your Chanel handbag on the terra-cotta; me in cut-offs and a ballcap.
Sand etched the sliding-door; sun bleached the mesa print bedspread.

I took your picture as you inhaled the desert willow, your failed
matrilineal insistence, too late for a daughter to demonstrate
acquiescence. That night at dinner your camera snapped
my tangled hair, a defiant wildness in my eyes, the taxonomy

of an unknown species—we are each losing our dreams,
at different hours in this smudged vortex of sage
and quartz. As I packed the car, you wandered down
the walk—to pluck a Fiddleneck—and reappeared,

stem stashed behind you ear, a yellow flower blooming.
You were humming. The sun seared the asphalt. We
simultaneously asked—Are you happy? Hands clasped,
we walked towards the car, on the verge of that canyon.

Dixie Cups

I never imagined that on the day I got married, my dead
mother would haul me off the street into an Episcopal Church,
as I jogged by early that morning. When I sit in the front-left pew,
the stained-glass sprinkles blue rosettes on the pulpit, she is beside

me, nestles her handbag on the hassock, shimmies her warm hand
from black leather glove, pats my bare knee. Her *Femme by Madame
Rochas* perfume mingles with candle wax and lilies. She adjusts
her periwinkle beret. How many Sundays did she pray with my father?

How many envelopes did she drop in the collection plate, alms
to her marriage? Those lonely Sundays, the dry wafers placed
in the palm of those who ate them—damp with their tears, their
bacon and eggs, fountain pen and after shave—she headed

to the rectory after church to drink with the clergy, the choir,
the vestry. When the Popov bottles were empty, and the moon
rose over the Potomac, she drove home across the Rochambeau
bridge, placed her purse in the foyer, and stuffed her beret

with the Sunday newspaper. She fetched a Dixie cup from
the bathroom, poured herself a nightcap, kissed us goodnight,
and went to bed. Decades of Sundays later, when I found
comfort in a Dixie Cup, my mother told me this: On the day I

was born, when she went into labor, she called my father's office
to tell him to meet her at the hospital. His colleague told her my
father was in a meeting with a big client. When my father showed
up three hours later, the doctor had performed a c-section; my mother

and I were asleep. My mother found a half-eaten box of Jujyfruits
from the matinee in his overcoat pocket a week later. She threw
them away and vacuumed the living room.

Pawn Shop Blues
~After Natasha Tretheway

I wiped my feet on the mat where the neon light shone.
Neon blinked pink at the threshold of "Things Silver and Gold".
My mother's silver smelled rusty, the pine box like mold.

When the jeweler looked up, his loupe'd eyes shone like a wolf.
When his hands reached for the box, I stepped back from the wolf.
The Pawn ends a life; his coin buffs death's gulf.

The Pawn unwrapped the flatware as I shifted my feet;
Handed me cash, while I shifted my feet.
I turned my face from my mother, left in retreat.

The path over yonder floods with tears
The yonder's wide canyon is full of tears
Though we mark time, the canyon is near.

I look in the windows at the spoons and knives.
My mother's face in the window, the eyes—they are mine.

Ode on a Carp

It's a long way around the Tidal Basin no matter
where you start you know how you are determined
to make up for these last two years when you sat

in your office gawked at that dried spider on your
window screen couldn't write got it in your head
that your resurrection as a person your path back

to normalcy to one of those push-up ice cream thingies
with orange sherbet and white ice cream in a cardboard
rocket is tied to peak bloom of the cherry blossoms because

of that picture on your desk you can't take your eyes off of
where you are three years old your mother holds you in front
of a row of cherry trees in DC you both are smiling you

even look cute with your tiny white gloves reaching out
towards the camera all of those curls tied up with a ribbon
that is probably pink the picture is black and white my mother

is still alive obviously we are happy I can't describe the red
of her lipstick but knowing my mother it is Revlon's
Cherries in the Snow pairs perfectly with the buds I have

made three sets of hotel reservations for early normal and late
bloom all refundable watched the National Park Service's
Bloom-Cam for weeks you might think I am desperate but

it's hope that there is a person I still like in here somewhere
here being my heart not the National Mall yesterday was peak
bloom today there are more people than blossoms which are getting

ripped from their pedicles by a cold wind I am glad for the
ventilation pass a guy wrapped in an American Flag poncho
he looks at my KN-95 mask turns to his friend who is drinking

a Schlitz says get a load of that freak so I rip off my mask
to ensure that he clearly hears me ask him what kind
of guy wears a poncho trust me I know ponchos go way back

to the Andes I actually love it when guys wear sarapes but that
isn't the point I tell my wife I am thinking of making a big scene
over it she says I already did we step over the mud slurry

from all of us tourists trampling the roots which makes me
think about being grounded I am not any more mostly since
January 6th but it's much bigger than that I will say anything

that pops into my head I am not sure what has happened
to my love of people suddenly I am in a crowd all of us
stopped looking at a guy fishing in the Tidal Basin his rod

as big as a pencil bending towards the Potomac he lets his
line out reels it in lets it out reels it in no one notices
the pink petals raining down on us like loaves

of bread not even me with my resurrection in process
we all watch the man until the fish surrenders you know
how they do when they quit swimming away from you

bloat on up to the water's surface let you haul them in
sideways almost floating there's the net waiting the guy is
beaming the crowd is cheering I am wondering what

this huge assed carp is doing chilling in the Tidal Basin
that's when I hear my mother laughing we are floating
at LumberLost under the waterfall she lets go of my hand
saying, *When you lose your self, you can find it downstream.*

The Ozarks

Poppett, my Poppett, catch me a thief.
Rub her with the juice of a walnut before I must sleep.
Somewhere past Branson, in the bank vault
   of history, my kin are ginning up again
On moonshine brewed in their root cellar, scrubbing
   ash crosses off their noble foreheads, shoving
Short pistols deep in the ribs of their neighborly
   bank tellers, my grandfather crashing
The safe's door, his hands smirched by walnuts;
   hungry Robin Hoods, eating bank failure and shale
Quarried from these ore forged bluffs; the limestone
   erosions made fortune's amputations
Possible. Nail a horseshoe to a walnut tree's stump;
   regrow your luck.

When I was five, I swiped a fire ball from
   Galena Seed and Feed, and my Granny
Dragged me up the courthouse stoop at high noon,
   made me sing to my doll with the elderberry eyes:
Poppett, my Poppett, catch me a thief.
Rub her with the juice of a walnut before I must sleep.
I don't know when we will have enough
   in this sinkhole between the James River
And these weeping caves. Watch us
   in the 1930's, weaving Jessie James dolls
From yellow hollyhock, baptizing them
   in the James River at moonrise, laying
Dreams like borrowed pennies
   on the tracks by the bridge, gifting
Fistfuls of stolen bills to our neighbors
   in the courthouse square, while the prisoners hum:
Poppett, my Poppett, catch me a thief.
Rub her with the juice of a walnut before I must sleep.

Here we are in the church by those tracks,
   our uncles at rest in the dust out back,
Sunlight streaming through the stained-glass Jesus,
   dust motes tumbling into the collection plate,
us exalting our good fortune, dropping
   our derringers into the cradles of young

Bonnies and Clydes waiting in line
    for the gun-fight ride at Silver Dollar City
As they case the place for the Branson Belle,
    faces hazy in the locomotive's steam, bandanas
Snug for the heist, hands at home, hooked into holsters,
    walnut juice staining our small pistoled palms,
Aching for one lucky break.

The Contextualist

My grandfather built the centerpiece of Galena, Missouri,
a graceful but practical courthouse of red brick, tricked
out with coffee shop and jail in its rounded rear. I can see
him grinding sandstone, his chiseled face caked with dust,

etching his name in the cornerstone. He always swings
his hammer as if swatting flies, and smiles at the ease
of his efforts. He seduced my grandmother who was
in nineth grade, just as women could vote, and he was laying

the cornerstone. My mother is unable to tell me if they
were in love or if it was convenience. I like to think
he saw a wild Ozark crow in the hook of her nose, heard
a dare in her laugh's shrill caw; that in her brown eyes

he saw himself reflected with a depth that surprised
him. I have been told that before a young crow leaves
its nest, it is white, and easy to spy. I imagine that he
was a magnetic, yet enigmatic, husband. He left her soon

after she had her third child. I have searched for proof
that my grandfather lived, besides my own existence.
No obituary exists; deny someone a grave and the lack
of an ending calls into question earlier chapters. He was

said to look like a movie star, was a wanderer; maybe he
was reckless. I tell myself he had an eye for calculations
and angles, that he was not casual. I can picture that cornerstone.

The Chinoiserie Wallpaper

Tonight, I am thinking about my grandmother's.
chinoiserie wallpaper in her living room, fern green
with peacocks. We used to sleep like two spoons on her
pullout sofa. The men in flat hats on her wall were bowed,
yoked to buckets of water; under the street light's glow,
the scene looked exotic. I was six, and the man from Sears

would come to your home, panting satchels of samples
up your front stairs, sweating Camel smoke, sprawl on your
pull-out, ask you what kind of look were you going for—
Orient, Confederate, Country Inn, or Garden Club? He had
my Granny pegged for Patriotic, since she told him she
worked on Capitol Hill, but she had travelled to Brazil, wanted

something expansive. I thought the wallpaper was the height
of glamorous, right out of Reader's Digest. And when my
Granny bought sheets for the pull-out that almost matched
the wallpaper, I couldn't sleep, tracing my index finger along
the peacock's plumage, the pagodas and pandas. Why do I
dream of that wallpaper even now? You are dead 35 years.

And that chinoiserie, we slept under its reductive Western Hemisphere
facsimile 60 years ago. I had not travelled as far as Connecticut, did
not understand oppression. You overflowed with laughter, opening
your umbrella in the foyer, grabbing my hand and your purse as we
headed to your office on Saturday. How is it that time has not faded
the paper, caused it to peel from the wall? As I pass from breath

into death will I step past the pull-out in your living room one
more time, will you take my hand along that path by the garden—
the one by the pond where the koi sleep under the lotus, where
the egret is singing, where you told me you'd wait if we were ever
separated?

The Panic Button

For my sixth birthday, my Granny took me to the Plaza Hotel
in New York City, just us, to see Eloise. As we rode the elevator

to the fifth floor, the Bellman pointed to the red panic button out
of my reach, told me that every kid in the city should know

what to do in a fire, a black-out, or a what-not. My Granny shushed
him, "Don't worry, honey. I will be here with you", and didn't I look

pretty in my pink birthday dress, cerise stripes, Nehru collar, fake
gold peace-sign necklace? At Afternoon Tea in the Plaza Hotel,

I was excited when Eloise and Skipperdee, her turtle who eats
raisins, came up to our table, but when she said, "I live on the

floor of the Plaza Hotel", I panicked. That evening at Hello Dolly,
I didn't sing along with Carol Channing. I scouted the Richard Rogers

Theater for fire escapes, sniffed for smoke, twisted my Peace necklace
in knots, asked if we could go back to the hotel. My Granny said, "Yes,

quit fretting", and we walked the mile back to the Plaza Hotel.
My Granny's asleep. Her left arm wraps around me as we snuggle

in one of the double beds in our Plaza Hotel room. I whisper over
and over, "If I should die before I wake, I pray the Lord my soul

to take." All of a sudden, my Granny touch types on my shoulder,
because she is a stenographer and she taught me too, "Angels watch

her through the night and keep her safe 'til morning light."
Lift me up, Angels, from the double bed in room 524 of the Plaza Hotel,

in New York City—I am the girl in the Eloise nightgown, eyes fixed
on the yellow velvet drapes, praying for sunrise, wishing she were braver—

a different granddaughter—not already grieving life
without her grandmother.

My Pattern of Habits

You know how your insight could use some insight
when you lie in corpse pose on the floor of your
office, listen to Lesson 5 of Unwinding Anxiety
and teacher quotes Alan Watts, says your being is nothing
but a pattern of habits—which gets you so triggered—sounds

ballistic, like a gun—not a feeling—funny how people never
say you are triggered by joy or love—people feel those—they
stockpile anger like ammo. I see that my being is hog slop.
My business went virtual, then virtually extinct. I took
on-line yoga every day—can do a side plank, let my hair

grow out gray—wash it every two to three days. It's not
like I guzzle a bottle of Chianti every night with dinner
or pound down dark chocolate when I write, as a rule.
You might wonder why I am gutted with guilt
about habits. Last night during my on-line writing class

my wife began vacuuming the hardwood floor over my head; I
wanted to stomp upstairs say "L B is teaching for God's sake—
I can't hear her—she will call on me when you are slinging
the sweeper". I texted my wife's cellphone KNOCK IT OFF,
knowing that she couldn't hear it, feeling an asshole's

satisfaction in a vacuum smack-down. How's that for
gratitude? I have lots of work to do on my spirit—which
I read today in the Atlantic is called anomie. I thought
that was French for no name—the author says it means
a lack of social connection that makes you act weird—

but he should have said bad, act very bad, when you
don't recall who you are or what matters because
you spend your days in your office unwinding anxiety
or going full Faulkner. I have become
insulter—oppressor—abuser—weapon, better than feeling

tenderness—which is hard when we have all lost
something. Where do I start with empathy? I lie
back down on the floor, make a list of things I am
thankful for—so corny, I am embarrassed to say them—
the Supreme Court letting me marry my wife, not

getting covid on Super Bowl Sunday two years ago
in that Ft. Lauderdale ER when I knocked myself out
on the Airbnb's sliding glass door, that anyone wants
to work in an ER, that I could remember my favorite
words after I clocked my head—like onomatopoeia and

flamingoes—that my grandmother who worked on Capitol Hill
for 40 years as a stenographer was dead on January 6—because
there is no shorthand for treason, full moons, Monet. Maybe
the cure for anomie is nomie—when you hum your name
like a hymn, whisper "Ann" like a psalm, worship who

you were, and you won't be again, but the gospel says
better. You recite it again and again in the night—like
your mother did when you woke up from a bad dream,
where you couldn't find your way home, and she held you
until the sun rose.

Ann Chinnis is an Emergency Physician of 40 years, a leadership coach, and CEO of her coaching business—Matrix Executive Coaching. As a New Year's resolution in 2017 (the only New Year's resolution she ever kept), Ann committed to rekindle her love for writing after a 40-year hiatus and enrolled in a beginning class at the Writers Studio in New York City. Ann has studied at the Writers Studio since that time and currently studies writing under Philip Schultz. Her poetry has been published in The Speckled Trout Review, Drunk Monkeys, Around the World: Landscapes & Cityscapes, Sledgehammer, Open Door, Last Leaves, Didcot Writers, the Sky Island Journal, Sheila-Na-Gig and Nostos. Ann and her wife live in Virginia Beach, Virginia.

www.ingramcontent.com/pod-product-compliance
Lightning Source LLC
Chambersburg PA
CBHW022107080426
42734CB00009B/1504